PAUSE REWIND PLAY

FUNDAMENTALS OF POSITIVE THINKING, A PRACTICE GUIDE TO EXPERIENCE THE UNTOLD SECRETS IN JUST 6 DAYS (HOW TO REPROGRAM SUBCONSCIOUS MIND)

LUCAS LENIN

Thank you for Choosing this Book and thanks to the universe for giving me an opportunity to bring it to your hand.

Contents

Preface

Congratulations, you've made the right decision to give yourself some of your precious time! And welcome to this joyful journey of discovering a new YOU!

- "What is Pause Rewind Play all about?"
- "Am I gonna learn something new?"
- "Is the reading experience gonna be life changing?"

Do these questions pop-up in your mind, as you hold the book in your hands? Please answer my questions before I address yours.

- Are you one of those having a tough time dealing with negative thoughts?
- Do you believe that developing positive thinking can work wonders in your life?
- Are you on your way to discovering yourself?

If your answer to these questions is YES, then I'm sure this book is gonna be of great support to you. You will become more conscious and mindful, develop a positive attitude and above all you are gonna learn the most important life skill – Mastering your mind, after you complete reading the book.

Do you think, just reading this book can bring in the changes that you expect to happen within you? Of course, NO. But YES, on a few conditions.

- SIX LIFE CHANGING DAYS

This book assigns you tasks for six days. Read a chapter in the morning and one in the evening, and practice the exercises taught there. Remember to read the book on six consecutive days. Don't give it a break.

- LITTLE DROPS OF WATER MAKE A MIGHTY OCEAN

Read the book, day by day and chapter by chapter. Don't attempt to read the whole book on the same day. Doing that, will make you miss the true essence of the book.

- PRACTICE MAKES PERFECT

Every topic that is reflected in this book, just gives you an awareness of who you are. The goal of this book doesn't stop at just helping you discover yourself but also mould you into the person that you wish to be. In order to make that happen, you need to follow the guidelines that are provided in each chapter and put them into practice. Not just practice, but SINCERE PRACTICE. I strongly believe that practice makes perfect. Agreed?

- TRAIN YOUR MIND

All the exercises that are suggested here are simple and are to train your mind. Hence, practicing them will definitely not affect your routine.

My valued reader,

I hope that you understand how to go about reading this book. Just dive in and enjoy the reward of discovering a new you.

PREFACE

This book helps people who Struggle to control the mind, Suffer with negative thoughts and Try to cultivate positive thoughts.

All the best!

CHAPTER ONE

FUNDAMENTALS FIRST

Day-1 Morning

"Who are you?"
Hello reader... The question is to you.
"Who are you?"

I heard you telling me your name. Do you think your name defines you the best? Your name is just to address you and not to define you.

Hold on... Did you tell me your educational qualification and profession? But these are some worldly possessions that you've earned.

My dear reader, the answer to the question, "Who am I?" is the most basic lesson, one should learn while attempting to understand and reprogram oneself. But the sad truth is that we always focus on the results rather than the basics. Hence, the first chapter throws light on this most basic life lesson.

Jog your memory to your past.

Do you remember the number of times you fell down, when you first learnt to ride the bicycle? Are you able to recollect and feel the nervousness that you had, when you drove your car on a busy street for the very first time? Did the hurt and anxiety, hold you from riding your bicycle or driving your car? Absolutely no. Then, how did you overcome those failures and anxiety? Initially, you would have needed time to understand the basics of driving – getting to know the different parts and the control you should have on them, in order to put the vehicle in proper motion. Once you mastered the basics and practised the skill regularly, you became a confident driver, didn't you?

Have you ever practiced breathing techniques, yoga, Alpha meditation or Zen meditation? Those are all techniques and methods that help us have a good mental health, ultimately to eliminate negative vibrations completely and to live with positive energy. But the sad truth is, from those all exercises you don't gain the expected result. Why? It's because you failed to understand and practice the basics of those techniques. Of course, the trainer would have taught you, but you didn't pay much attention to it.

Beware reader! Let's not commit the same mistake again. So, Fundamentals First!

"Who are you?"

You are a soul – a separate invisible element that dwells in your body. And your thought is the language of your soul and consciousness. Hence, for a person to be called alive and conscious, his brain needs to generate thoughts.

Your soul, your body and your thoughts are three inseparable separate elements that are present in you. But, when a person dies, his soul and thoughts just leave his body. That's why we wish the soul to Rest In Peace, whereas the buried body gets decomposed.

It's really really important for a person to feed all these three elements – soul, body and thoughts.

We eat thrice a day and hence our body gets fed. We also do some exercises to have a good physique. But, what about our soul and thoughts? Do we feed them regularly? Yes, we do, but we are not conscious about it. When we read a book or watch a movie, we are actually feeding our thoughts.

What you speak and listen are for your thoughts,

What you eat and drink are for your body.

Now you have an awakening in your conscious mind, but this has to get registered in your subconscious mind. Here's how you can do that.

- Say the statement, "Body, thoughts and I are separate", in your mind (if you say it aloud, your friends might mock at you).
- Repeat it once in every fifteen minutes or half an hour.

- Initially, you can also set an alarm to keep yourself reminded of the task.
- The more you make this affirmation, the more strongly it gets etched in your subconscious mind.

That's it. Simple. Is the task as hard as lifting a 100 kg weight, or running 5 km a day to reduce your belly? No, not at all. It's as simple as swiping your mobile screen. This simple task requires a sincere effort. Do follow the guidelines provided above and register the most basic lesson in your subconscious mind.

It's a usual day for those around you. But, for you, it's a red letter day. You're practicing the first and most basic life lesson.

Stays connected and continue the exercise throughout the day. Let's meet tonight.

Action Plan: Write the statement *"Body, Thoughts and I are separate" 12 times.*

1.
2.
3.
4.
5.
6.
7.
8.
9.
10.
11.
12.

Day 1 - Evening

How was the practice?

If you had done the exercise with full involvement, and shown certain sincerity, if you had done it passionately, then, by this time that sentence would definitely be lingering in your mind. Kudos! You are on the right track.

If you think that you could barely practice the exercise because of your busy schedule, no problem. Set an alarm to remind you of the practice and try to fall on track. But please don't give up.

Whenever you pick up your phone, read the messages and respond to them, tell yourself that this is because of your thoughts. Every time you feed your tummy, just register in your mind that this is for your body.

When you continue the same practice for a couple of days, over a period of time your concentration will improve. You can't improve your concentration on anything without consistent practice even if you spend thousands of money. When you do it regularly, your subconscious mind believes and it will get registered there. After a couple days when you wake up in the morning, your mind starts reciting the mantra "Body, thoughts and I are separate".

When this happens, be sure that your subconscious mind has already received and registered the mantra. Now you have experienced only the overview of it. When you do it repeatedly, it will go into a deeper level of subconsciousness.

So, what if this statement gets deeper into your subconscious mind? What are you gonna gain out of it?

Believe me or not, this simple statement helps you learn one of the most important skills - self control. Let me explain you, how.

Imagine that you are an ardent lover of Mercedes. Every time you see it somewhere, you just fall in love instantly and you start yearning to own it. In spite of possessing a branded car yourself, you are tempted to go for the Mercedes. You might also make efforts to purchase it without considering your financial situation. Eventually you might end up in a financial crisis. But my friend, don't worry. You are definitely not gonna be a victim of this pathetic situation because; you have already become the master of your thoughts. So hereafter, you are gonna place your needs before your wants and make careful decisions.

Do you really like to get a piece of mind from others on financial matters? How do you feel when someone advises you not to spend money on this and that? What would be your reaction when someone holds your hand when you are about to take the first bite of your favorite pizza, telling you that it is unhealthy? Definitely your ego doesn't like others poking their nose into your matters. Right ?

Worry not, my friend. As you have now become the controller of your thoughts, you need no adviser to help you on any matter. Before you consume a junk food or spend money on your wants, you receive a warning from your thoughts. That awakening is so important and you have already gained it. Continue the same practice and repeat it. When you continue the practice, you start feeling the calmness in mind; automatically reducing the unwanted noise inside your mind. Reciting this mantra, "Body, Thoughts and I are separate", must become your habitual action. Believe that this practice will bring in the desired changes in your life and it will definitely happen. When you wake up tomorrow morning, you must be able to observe the mantra being hummed in your mind. All the best!

Have a good sleep; I will see you tomorrow morning.

CHAPTER TWO

3 STATES OF MIND

Day 2 - Morning

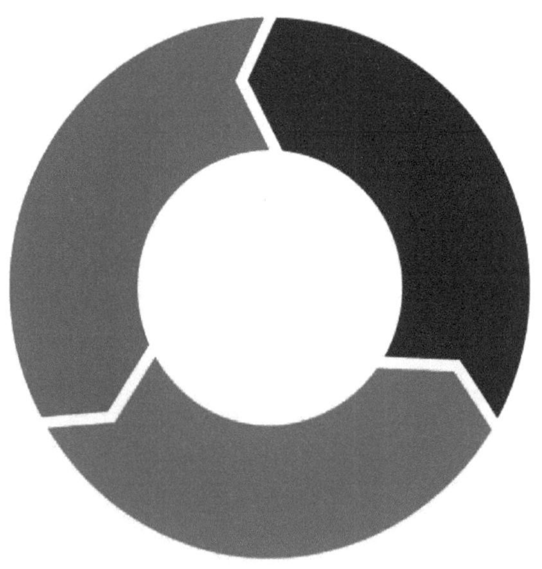

One day, on the earth, at 5 a.m. ...

Mr. A : Dear God, you know that today is really a significant day to me. I'm awaiting a promotion. I strongly believe that you'd not forsake me. Please grant me that promotion. I believe that I've already got my wish granted and thank you from the depth of my heart.

In heaven...

God (to Himself) : How great his trust is! I'm truly impressed. I must grant him his wish and make his prayers come true.

The same day, at 10 a.m. ...

Mr.A arrives at the office, greets everyone and feels more elated than ever.

Mr.B : Hello Mr.A. You look so enthusiastic today. Let me guess the reason behind your excitement. Mmmmm... I got it. Today is promotion day and your name is on the top of the list.

Mr.A : Exactly Mr.B. Who else in this office deserves the promotion than I?

Mr.B : Of course, you are the most deserving. But Mr.A, don't count your chickens before they hatch. Didn't Mr.C, the most meritorious employee, miss his promotion last year?

Mr.A (to himself) : What if he is right? What if I don't get my promotion? Should I wait for another year for my promotion or apply for a new job where I get paid more?

God : ?????????

Hey there! Welcome to the second day of our journey. I hope, you can easily relate yourself to the scenario narrated above.

What would you do, if you were the God?

Would you grant him his wish?

Wouldn't the contradiction between his thoughts and actions, confuse you?

Of course, it would.

My dear reader, this kind of situation is quite common in all our lives. We strongly believe something in our conscious mind, but some hidden thoughts from our unconscious mind always put us in a state of dilemma and eventually we get stuck up.

Today's lesson teaches you how to watch your thoughts and get rid of those what ifs. Before we begin, I'd like you to know the three states of mind – Conscious, Unconscious and the Subconscious- and their functions, especially about the Conscious and Unconscious minds – the widely misunderstood concepts.

Imagine that you are reading a book. If both your eyes and mind read the book, then you are in a conscious state. But if only your eyes read and your mind takes a diversion, and gets obsessed with a thought or an incident that happened in the past, then it is your unconscious mind that is active. You don't do it purposefully. But it happens.

When your mind is engaged in something without any distractions, your attention is completely focused on the core job, work, project or entertainment and is called the conscious mind.

When your mind gets obsessed with thoughts from the past or about the future, then your attention gets disturbed and the unconscious mind takes up the control and influences the conscious mind.

It doesn't matter whether the conscious or the unconscious mind takes up the control. What actually matter are the thoughts that keep flowing in your mind. Gautama Buddha states, " What you think, you become". Our thoughts are very powerful than we can imagine. It needs tremendous practice to keep our thoughts organized and positive.

Try to visualize this scenario. There are two students preparing for their final exams. The first one makes the affirmation, “ I must pass”. Whereas the latter keeps telling himself, “I mustn’t fail”. Whom do you think passes the exam? Obviously, it is the one who wants to pass the exam and definitely not the one who doesn’t want to fail.

Have you heard people lament about things that don’t happen the way they expect them to be? Their expectations must have been close to come true, but they just missed. Why?

Having a better understanding about the conscious and unconscious minds, helps you figure out the answer to your why.

I have a task for you. Take a piece of paper and list down the worries that occupy your mind and the problems that you face every day.

- I’m not happy in my relationship.
- I work hard but I don’t make enough money.
- I have health issues.
- I find it a big challenge to attract customers to my business.
- I’m not able to put up with things that happen at my work place.
- I’m short tempered.
- I lost a huge amount of money in my business.
- I really study hard but I fail in the exams.
- I don’t have a government job.
- I’m not in good terms with my in-laws.
- I’m not able to earn good friends.

Does your list resemble the one above? There would definitely be a few or some or almost all or more than this in your list of worries. Your past experiences or memories have caused these worries and they have already got registered in your unconscious mind. These are the thoughts that distract you. SO, how often do they appear in your mind? Let's do a rough calculation. If you were a person who cares about your physical and mental health, then a day in your life would be scheduled like this.

- 5 minutes for meditation
- 10 minutes for affirmation
- 15 minutes for visualization
- 30 minutes for exercise
- 7 hours for sleep

On an average you spend 8 hours for your wellness and carry out your routine for the remaining 16 hours. It is during this time, when you try to engage yourself in an activity that these worries from your unconscious mind pop up and refrain from carrying out your work. It also drains all the energy that you possess. So, I'm gonna suggest an exercise that will help you monitor your thoughts and organize them.

Every once in a while stop doing the activity that you're engaged in, read your thoughts and then proceed with your task. For instance, stop for a moment, while preparing breakfast. Ask yourself, "What was I thinking?" Elicit the answer and then carry on with cooking. When you are busy preparing a report, stop, read your thoughts and proceed. Try to watch your thoughts every fifteen or thirty minutes. It is said that, every day, around 60000 plus thoughts are generated in our mind. If you can perform this exercise sincerely, then you'll definitely be able to monitor your thoughts at least 30 times a day, which is just 0.0005 % of the total thoughts generated.

Attention dear reader! Monitor only the unconscious thoughts and not the conscious ones. If you do this exercise with full commitment and spirit, then you can monitor 100-200 thoughts.

Best of luck with the new activity!

Let's meet tonight. Have a great day.

Action Plan: Write 21 unconscious thoughts you noticed throughout the day.

1.
2.
3.
4.
5.
6.
7.
8.
9.
10.
11.
12.
13.
14.
15.
16.
17.
18.
19.
20.
21.

Day 2 - Evening

Hello! How do you do? How was your day?

Were you able to carry out the assigned task? How many thoughts were you able to monitor? At least 30 of them?

Bravo! You've done a great job.

Now, let me tell you, in what way this exercise can help you mould yourself.

If you had monitored your thoughts keenly, you would have noticed that most of them are unwanted and bring no meaning to your life. All these days you had been carried away by these unwanted anxieties, fears and many other such emotions presented to you by Mr.Unconscious Mind. But, from now on, you are not gonna let this happen to you because, you have already fixed a CCTV to monitor your thoughts. So, how is this CCTV gonna work and yield the result you expect?

Imagine, you're beginning a new day. You wake up with a lot of positive energy and enthusiasm. While carrying out your morning routine, an unwanted thought from your unconscious mind peeps in. Watch out my friend! Don't let this unwanted, unconscious thought spoil your day. So, how would you handle it? Quite simple. Stop the task you're carrying out, for a moment. Ask yourself, "What was I thinking?" Be vigilant and monitor your thoughts. If it is one of those useless thoughts, say no to it immediately. Then your unconscious unwanted thoughts will get disconnected and you become conscious.

What if, a person who hasn't learnt to observe his thoughts, comes across the same situation? When his unconscious mind picks up some unwanted thoughts, he would just travel with them the whole day. He neither acts mindfully nor does proper justification to the work he does throughout the day. Eventually, the whole day gets spoiled.

Do you know why is it that only less than 2% of people are super successful in this world? Because they are the master of their mind and they know how to handle it. I assure you, if you practise this exercise regularly, you will start analyzing your thoughts and stop thinking about unwanted thoughts in your life. Ultimately, you too will become a successful person.

Dear reader, the key to success (observing your thoughts) is in your hands now. When you use it for the first time, it might be a little difficult for you. But, the more you use it, the more you get used to it and the doorways to success is always open for you. Remember, your thoughts design your future. Monitoring and channelizing them is really important.

When you're dragged away by an unwanted thought, just Stop, Ask, Say No and Proceed.

I'll talk to you in the next chapter. Good night.

CHAPTER THREE

3 HEROES

Day 3 Morning

Hello! Welcome to the third day of our expedition.

But, before we give it a start, here's a quick glance and reminder on the objectives of the joy-filled journey that we are on. You are now half way through the process of discovering and transforming yourself to the person you have always wished to be. Though we call it a joyful journey, it has its own challenges and obstacles. To introspect and understand oneself is not as easy as it is said. It needs consistent efforts, perseverance and focus to reach your destination. I'm really happy that you are strong and focused enough to take up the task. Keep up the spirit and the smart work. All the best!

Let's now dive into today's learning. Have you ever wondered about the way our body and mind function? Of course, we do know the functions of our body and its different organ systems. But, what about the mind? As its functions are very subtle, it's quite challenging for us to understand. Today's lesson casts light on the three silent but powerful heroes of our body – the mind, the sense and the ego.

The mind:

The mind is the place where thoughts are generated based on one's experience. It receives inputs from the five sense organs and interprets them. The mind makes you react quickly. Sometimes we say or do something without thinking about it. It is good sometimes; but most of the times, doing something without thinking about it, lands us in difficult situations.

Imagine, there is a bowl of hot water. When you place your hand in it, you immediately sense the heat energy and take off your hand. What actually happens in this situation is that, the mind receives an input from the nerves that connect your hand and brain. Then, it passes a command back to the hand to remove it from the hot water. Here, the quick reaction, actually works.

Let's consider another situation. During school days, most of the students get affected by Mathsophobia – fear of Mathematics. Sometimes, even the class topper gets affected by this phobia. Do you know why? Perhaps, the student had difficulty understanding the number concept or he/she had gone through a situation in the past where he/she was humiliated in front the whole class for not performing well in Maths. This past experience gets registered in the mind and influences the present decision made by the mind. The very word Maths threatens such students and the mind tells them, " Hey! It's Mathematics. It's not your cup of tea. You can never become good at it." In this context, the quick reaction doesn't work out. It just lets you down.

The sense:

As the name suggests, the sense is always sensible. Unlike the mind, it always makes sensible decisions and not emotional decisions. It answers all your whys and hows. It usually takes time to analyse a situation and helps you make better decisions. Unfortunately, these decisions also are influenced by past experiences. But luckily, interference of the past experiences and memories can be removed, by practising meditation and positive affirmations.

Let's consider the same situation discussed under, the mind. If a student with Mathsophobia allows the sense to analyse things, then he might be able to overcome the phobia and excel at Maths. The sense would tell him, " Hey! Don't let your past experience influence you. If you can be good at Science, why can't you do well in Maths? May be you need to spend some more time to let the number concept get registered. You can also get some help from your Maths teacher. Don't give up. Work smart and you'll definitely be able to learn this subject with ease."

The sense makes sure that your past experiences don't influence your present decisions. It helps you make wise decisions.

The ego:

The ego is actually how you perceive yourself and others perceive you. When you let your ego make choices, it does it in such a way that it holds the perception true.

Do you remember the question that I asked you in the first chapter, “Who are you?”? I have also given you the answer there.

Yes, the soul, your true self has the right to rule you. So, quieting the ego is really important, so that the soul takes control.

My valued reader, while making efforts to reprogram our subconscious mind, we must also gain knowledge and proper understanding of these three invisible elements – the mind, the sense and the ego- in our body. Please don’t feel confused about the terms that are used here. What we’re actually aiming to achieve is to monitor and organize our thoughts, for, “You become what you think.” It may sound simple. But it needs tremendous effort and a keen focus to make it happen.

Take a look at how these three elements play their role when a below demonstrated situation arises.

Imagine you had an argument with your boss because; you had a difference of opinion while deciding on a matter last week. Today, when you are in a meeting with your boss with all the other colleagues, your unconscious mind suddenly picks up the thought about the same argument. At this situation, if the three invisible elements make a conversation with you, then it would be something like this.

The mind : Hey you, don’t ever think of opening your mouth. Your boss never listens to you.

You : Yes, you’re right. I’m not gonna give any of my suggestions and opinions in today’s meeting.

The sense : (Untrained) Remember, the last time, the discussion with your boss turned into an argument because, he was not ready to accept your ideas.

(You're a genuine person and have always worked sincerely for your company. You're not able to hold yourself. When you're about to give in, your ego will begin a conversation with you.)

The ego : He insulted you and yelled at you in front of everybody. Have you forgotten? If you present your ideas in this meeting, what will your colleagues think of you? Won't that spoil your image? Keep your mouth shut.

This happens in your subtle body. Now if you're trained to monitor your thoughts you can

handle this situation so easily.

You'll have to do just three things : PAUSE, REWIND and PLAY.

When the three rulers give you their suggestions, just PAUSE your thoughts. REWIND and read

them carefully. If you think that those thoughts make a negative influence, then you'll have to

pass on these commands to the three kings:

To the mind: Hey Mr.Reactive, Stay calm. Don't pick up any negative thoughts.

To the sense: Hello Mr.Sensible, don't let my past experience influence you. Try to give me some sensible and productive suggestions. Never ever agree with everything that the mind says. Please analyse the situation carefully and suggest me some good ideas.

To the ego : Hey Mr.Ego, I wanna be myself. I'd like to be true to myself. Don't try to act smart and influence the mind and the sense.

Now PLAY. You'll definitely make wise decisions.

So, let's begin today's exercise. Today's practice is not much different from yesterday's practice. Yesterday you just monitored your unconscious thoughts. Today, we're gonna add one more step to it – analyse your thoughts. When you're engaged in a task, just pause and ask yourself, "What was I thinking?" Then analyse the thought. Check whether the thought is about past or future and negative or positive thought. That's it.

You have a full day, start your exercise, pause in-between unconscious thoughts, rewind and check what you were thinking and play. Show your fullest sincerity in doing this exercise and take control of your most valuable invisible tools.

Let's meet tonight. Have a good day.

Action Plan : Write 21 unconscious thoughts you noticed throughout the day and write past or future, also positive or negative

1.
2.
3.
4.
5.
6.
7.
8.
9.
10.
11.
12.
13.
14.
15.
16.

17.
18.
19.
20.
21.

Day 3 - Evening

How was the exercise?,

If you had done the practice sincerely every half an hour, you'd have monitored at least 30 unconscious thoughts. This is the first step towards reprogramming your subconscious mind. So far nobody has ever questioned the three invisible elements in you. First time as a soul you tried to rule and control your mind. How was the feeling when had a conversation with them? Did you enjoy it? I'm sure that the experience would have been a new feeling to you. That real 100% feeling you can't experience within a day, practice daily. Ask them questions regularly.

When I say ruling your inner tools and mind, you might think dominating and ruling is negative. But you are trying to take control over them in a positive way, which you need to understand. How you take care of your car, how you take care of your mobile phone without any scratch, like that you need to take more control of your subconscious tools - Mind, sense and ego. With the help of those tools only we are going to achieve biggest things in our life. You needn't get angry and shout at them, but politely advise them not to speak unwanted thoughts. Your soul is the hero, it has to act and show heroism.

Do You know what sort of benefit you get from this practice? You might have heard the statement, "*what you think, you become*". Today, the whole day you asked questions to your mind, sense and ego. When you continue the same practice, over a period of time, your mind doesn't pick unwanted thoughts, your senses don't feed further thoughts, your ego doesn't say any more yes to them. They will remain like well disciplined children, and wait for your order. If you want to draw a painting, the mind will give you creative ideas and sense will give related additional inputs.

When your mobile phone frequently hangs, you erase unwanted files and erase junk folders and try to make it perfect. Maximum you do factory reset. That's what we are doing with the help of ego, not allowing to generate any more negative thoughts. When you think a thought continuously for 17 seconds, it starts to align with the frequency of the universe, it will start manifesting. That's why whenever your unconscious thoughts activate, you must act really fast and question your inner tools, so that you can stop the thought process within 5 or 10 seconds. Then how come negative thoughts start to manifest in your life?

Imagine for a moment, you love to eat sweets.

Your mind would say, "wow sweets".

Your sense will feed, "hey this is so tasty, last time you missed. Come on, take it and taste it.

Your ego will alert you, "hey, they are asking for sweet. Before your hand picks that sweet, you yourself decide that sweet is not good for health. Say no."

Earlier you were tempted to eat without any control, now you have gained self control.

In Life, during every transition, you purify yourself.

It's a nature of these 3 inner tools, invisible elements,

The nature of mind is to pick at something related to the 5 senses -Smell, Sight, Touch, hearing, Taste. These all 5 senses are connected to emotions.

Imagine for a moment, you're cross a flower shop or seeing someone presenting a bouquet to his girlfriend. You senses of smell and sight get triggered. Immediately, you start imagining any of your past or future experience.

You are walking on the road, there is a Black BMW car coming towards you fast, the eye sees the car coming fast, mind picks thought, senses feed and start guessing how fast the car is coming towards you and how to protect you. Here fear and nervousness are the feelings. Imagine for a moment, when you see black BMW even after one month from the incident, your mind picks up old thoughts, senses start feeding how horrible that whole day was.

Let's take an example: you start a discussion with one of your friends about business matters. While speaking your friend acknowledges your ideas by saying ok or nodding his head. Have you noticed? If your friend does not express his acknowledgement, it means that he is not listening. Then you stop to speak. That's what ego does exactly. Every time the mind picks some thought, sense feeds on and on, and ego will acknowledge. Now you have gained self control, ego will never say anymore ok. It has learnt to be assertive. How? You've started to question them. Wow, super, lovely, beautiful. That's the nature of mind, we can't change. But we can control them, by telling them, what they should do and what they shouldn't do.

Have you heard people telling?

"Will you please use your mind?,

"Do you have any sense?"

"Don't be an egotistical person."

Where is that mind, sense, ego? That's what we are discussing now. The ego is the biggest enemy to all, that's why we are taking control of ego first; we are nominating ego as supervisor here. Then no need to fear the thief. Because, ego itself is the thief. It accepts anything and everything proposed by the sense. It doesn't let you play your role. When you stop accepting everything that is fed by the sense, the latter will get stunned and wait for the ego's response. Ego's duty now is to report about the conversation to you. Now you'd interfere and inquire them about the conversation. That's it.

How did you register the first day's affirmation in your mind? Do you hear that affirmation being hummed in your mind? The same way try to talk your inner tools and bring them under your control.

Continue the practice every 15 minutes or half an hour once, until you go to bed. Create a new cycle to purify your thoughts.

We'll meet tomorrow morning. Good night.

CHAPTER FOUR

SILENCE

Day 4 - Morning

Happy morning! I wish you a good day.

Today, just for a change, we're gonna begin our lesson with a simple activity to our brain. Here we go!

Rearrange all the letters of the given words and make new words.

Eg: LEMON - MELON

SAINT - ____________

EARTH - ____________

MARCH - ____________

SUPER - ____________

LISTEN - SILENT

Kudos! I hope your brain box was kept busy and engaged with the above activity. The answers for the exercise are provided at the end of this chapter

Listen and Silent, the last pair of words in the above list, is gonna be our topic of discussion.

Rewind your memory. Travel back to your school days. Can you recollect a scenario similar to the one described below?

This happened during my school days. I was in my ninth grade. We were 50 of us in the class. We used to have a lot of fun during every break. Not only breaks, but also in the absence of a teacher during class hours. Our principal was a very strict man. Nobody dared to even face him. One fine day, our Maths teacher was late to the class. We didn't want to miss that time. We started yelling, shouting and running around the classroom. Suddenly, our principal entered our classroom. He called out our class leader and shouted at him for being so irresponsible. We were then severely punished by him. He also stated that, that was the last warning for us. From then on we became very alert. Just when we heard his footsteps we would settle down in our places and behave well.

So, why have I narrated this to you? In what way is it connected to our topic of discussion? Let me clarify it.

Dear reader, just recall all the exercises that you have been since day one of our program. The first day, you registered in your subconscious mind that "Body, Thoughts and I are separate." The second day, you just monitored your thoughts. On the third day, you went a step ahead and had a conversation with the three invisible heroes of your body. So, what you actually did on the third day was that every time your mind picked up a thought, you interfered and interacted with your mind, sense and ego. You instructed them what to do and what not to do, like our principal warned us. From today onwards your duty is gonna be quite simple. You are just going to peep in to your mind to listen to the thoughts it has picked up. But you won't hear anything. Why? Because, you have already instructed them their dos and don'ts, as our principal did to us. Hereafter, just your presence will make all the difference. You need not spend your energy talking to the three kings. That sounds really simple!

Yes, this is what you're gonna do the whole day today.

Imagine, you're cutting vegetables and your mind picks up a thought from the past. You get distracted. If this had happened yesterday, you would have PAUSED, REWINDED and PLAYED your thoughts. But today, your task is very simple. You just PAUSE to listen to your thoughts. Do you think you'll hear them speak? No, not at all. Your mind, sense and ego have become aware that you are monitoring them. You've also made it clear that they are not supposed to pick up any negative thoughts. So, they won't dare to do what they used to do. Now your soul is learning its role as the ruler. Congratulations! You have identified the silent ruler who had been dwelling within you since your birth.

Never ever let your ruler get down the throne. Then you'll witness miracles in your life.

You just try to LISTEN as many times as possible and they will become SILENT.

Let's meet tonight. Have a great day ahead.

Answers to the exercise given in the beginning of the chapter.

SAINT - STAIN

EARTH - HEART

MARCH - CHARM

SUPER - PURSE

Day 4 - Evening

Hello and welcome back!

How well did you play your role as a headmaster to your invisible heroes? What was their response? Did they remain silent when you tried listening to them? Did you enjoy that moment of silence?

If yes, pat yourself. You're really amazing!

How many times did you peep in to your mind to observe it? At least 20 times? Great! Try to listen to the three invisible elements as many times as possible. Because, the more you listen, the more silent moments you can cherish.

So, what kind of change in your behavior pattern can you observe after practicing this exercise?

Observe these two pictures.

There are two kinds of alarm setters, To which category do you belong?

Even if you had been in the second category, you wouldn't remain there anymore. As your soul has taken up the role of the ruler it will never let your mind control you. When the alarm goes at 7 a.m. and your body demands few more minutes of sleep, the response is gonna be 'No'. Your soul will pass the command to your mind and it has to obey. There is no other go! So far the mind and body had been controlling you. But now, you have taken control over them. Hereafter you will wake up in the morning even without any alarm.

If a day's practice of this exercise can yield you such a great reward, then imagine the result of practicing it every day for a year. You would be filled with a lot of energy, enthusiasm and optimism. You would become thoughtful, conscious and mindful. Isn't that wonderful?

Do you know why 95% of people live a mediocre lifestyle? It's because, they are totally unaware of these techniques to control their mind. Instead of them being rulers, they have let the three kings rule them and they have always been their slaves. But super successful people live only on conscious thought and they are only 2% in the total population of the world.

My treasured reader, at present, you are in the transformation zone. You're getting shifted from the mediocre lifestyle (90%) to successful (7%) then super successful (3%). My best wishes to you.

The optimism and energy that you have gained are super contagious. Your mind, sense and ego, and the ones who surround you also pick them up. Hence, instead of feeding you with negative thoughts, all the three heroes will also become optimistic and give you productive ideas. So, you're gonna be the source and secret of optimism and enthusiasm of people around you. People would love hanging out with you.

Practising meditation and making affirmations will definitely be fruitful, because you are now the boss and you have learnt to focus on your conscious thoughts. No more negative thoughts or thoughts from your unconscious mind can distract you anymore.

Keep practicing! Success is only a few steps ahead of you.

Good night. I'll meet you tomorrow.

CHAPTER FIVE

Positive Vibration

Day 5 - Morning

"Take a deep breath. Inhale peace; exhale happiness."

Hello reader! I cordially welcome you to the fifth day of our program.

Any guess about today's topic of discussion? Yes, you're right. Today's lesson throws light on "Breathing and its significance."

Before we begin, here's a task for you.

Place your hand on your belly.

Take a deep breath through your nose.

Hold it for a few seconds.

Exhale.

Repeat it for five times. Just observe your breath. Are you done?

Now, answer my question. When you inhaled, did your belly move in or move out? Did it move out? Good job! It means that your breathing is proper.

Proper breathing starts in the nose and then moves to the stomach as your diaphragm contracts, the belly expands and your lungs fill with air. Unfortunately, some of us don't do it properly. As breathing is a kind of a reflex action, we fail to observe it and hence everything goes wrong. In today's lesson we're going to learn to observe our breath and also gain knowledge on the benefits that we acquire by doing so.

Recall the first day's exercise. I had instructed you to make the affirmation, "Body, thoughts and I are separate."

Though these three are separate, they are inter connected. As your soul dwells in your body, the latter's existence is really important for the former to carry out its duties. So, how do you know that your body is alive? The easiest way to tell that is to check one's breathing. When a person stops breathing, his body dies and his soul leaves the body. Hence, breathing determines one's existence but, proper breathing determines one's life. There's a huge difference between existing and living. In order to live your life, you need to take very good care of your body, mind and soul. And that's what we have been doing for the past four days. After your strenuous efforts, you have made it to the position of the ruler of yourself. That's really appreciable. Practising the exercises regularly will help you retain the position. So keep practicing.

Now, let's get back to the subject of discussion today, "Breathing". Here's what I want you to do to make your breathing proper and gain the benefits. Just add another step to yesterday's exercise. Yesterday, you played the role of a headmaster to the three invisible heroes in you and made sure that they didn't get involved in unnecessary talks. Today, go a step ahead and observe your breath too.

Imagine, you're washing the clothes. Pause. Peep in to your mind and monitor the thoughts. Are you able to experience silence? Enjoy that silence for a few seconds. Now, come back and observe your breath for some time. Inhale and exhale; inhale and exhale. Get back to your work. Observing your breath can help you improve your concentration.

Practices like yoga and meditation need a lot of concentration. When there's a lot of chaos in your mind, do you think you can focus on what you do? Impossible. But now, that you have taken absolute control of yourself; you can obtain that concentration, effortlessly.

There's also a very significant advantage of monitoring your thoughts and observing your breath. When you monitor your thoughts, you are actually purifying your thoughts and living consciously. Every time you observe your breath, you are actually helping your body produce all positive cells. You know that cells are the basic elements of our body. There are about 724 trillion cells in our body.

Every single second a million cells die and at the same time a million cells are born. Now, my dear friend, when you remain optimistic and start observing your breath, you are in fact, helping your body produce cells that are filled with optimism and a lot of energy. Imagine what would happen if you can practice the exercises for 50 times or 100 times a day. You would become a positive, vibrant magnet. You would become a great source of positive energy. Wouldn't it be wonderful? So, what are you waiting for?

Go, Monitor your thoughts and Observe your breath. Obtain as much positive energy as you can from the universe.

All the best!

I'll talk to you tonight.

Day 5 - Evening

Hey there! What's up?

I'm sure that you'd have enjoyed experiencing the moment of silence in your mind and observing your breath. It gives me immense pleasure to meet an optimistic and energetic person, You.

Mr/Ms. Optimistic, you know what? People witnessing your success are definitely gonna envy you, for being so lucky. But I tell you, it's not your luck but the consistent effort and hard work that you put in, are behind this remarkable success. Keep up your spirit and energy, and achieve great things in your life.

When a person gets trained to do things consciously, his life starts changing the way he wants it to be. Imagine, you make a lot of money, but still you lead a mediocre life.

Why? It's because of the long list of expenditures. Only when you work on your expenditure and differentiate your needs from wants, you can save up some money and take your life to the next level. The same thing applies for the generation of thoughts also. On one hand, you make sincere efforts like practicing yoga and meditation to generate positive thoughts. On the other hand, your mind picks up negative thoughts from your unconscious mind and keeps accumulating them. Eventually, there's going to be no difference in your life. You are gonna remain the same person you used to be.

When you are losing all your energy for negative thought, then where will you find energy to work for positive thought and live in the conscious mind? When your unconscious mind stops producing thoughts from mind, then the entire energy flow will support the conscious mind.

Now finally, after 5 days of tiring efforts, you have reprogrammed your subconscious mind. Now you are like a boss, instructing and leading your mind. Here after, your mind will act as per your instructions. Kudos!

Continue to PAUSE, REWIND and PLAY and achieve greater things in your life.

Let's meet tomorrow morning. Good night.

CHAPTER SIX

True Power in You

Day 6 - Morning

I vividly remember the day I got fired from a high paid job, because I had started a business for an additional income. My company used to pay me $1350 per month and my business gave me an income of $450. Everything was going on well until one day my higher authority called me and said, “You are fired”. I felt awful but I didn’t give up. I started paying more attention to the business I had started. My consistent efforts began yielding me the rewards that I expected. I took up the revenue from $2000 per month to $16000 per month. I was happy to earn $3000 as profit. Unfortunately, our business started going downhill. The income was as low as $4000 per month. I was devastated. I lost all my hope. Then finally, I decide to take up a job in a company. I started looking for opportunities but in vain. “How nice would it be if I were offered a job in the same company from where I was fired?” I started thinking. It was at that moment my life started changing. My journey turned into spirituality.

My most valued reader, on this sixth and final day of our program I’m gonna share with you two important secrets that worked miracles in my life. I’m gonna tell you how I made my thoughts come true; how I recognized the true power in me; how I trained my subconscious mind and made more money. Stay with me till the end, learn the secrets and wait for miracles to happen in your life.

After the huge loss in my business I decided to work for a company. I wished I were recruited by the same company that fired me. To make my wish come true I followed two techniques – Powerful Affirmation and Powerful Visualization. Here’s what I did. I started making the affirmation, “I’m so happy and grateful for getting my job back in the same company”. I repeated the sentence at an intense level for 5 minutes every morning. Following the affirmation I practised visualization. I visualized like I walked into the company with a lot cheer and enthusiasm and accepted the offer with a grateful heart. I repeated visualizing the scene for 5 times. I practised these two techniques very sincerely for just three days. On the 4th day, around 6:45 a.m. I received a call from my boss, who fired me. He told me that the company had decided to make an offer to me again and that the HR would call me shortly. I couldn't believe my ears. Finally, I got a job in the same company with a higher pay.

If these two techniques could work wonders in my life why can't they to you? Here's the proper method to practice these techniques. Learn it well, apply it in your life and witness wonders.

Powerful Affirmation

Sit comfortably on a flat surface (If you can, do Bhastrika Asana). Close your eyes and take deep breath thrice. Try to concentrate on the space between two eyebrows.This concentration point is called as Third Eye or Glabella point or Yintang point. There are 7 Chakra points in our body. But we are able to imagine, visualize and feel only the Third eye, which is the powerful intuition, sense of purpose and direction of life. The other 6 points can't be visualized exactly.

Your eyes and mind are required to concentrate on that point, and start saying your affirmation for a minute, then 2nd day 2 minutes, 3rd day 3 minutes and so on. Gradually increase the time and start saying the affirmation at least for 5 minutes every single morning. Keep the affirmation statement as simple as possible. Don't make it too long.

Powerful Visualization

Sit comfortably on a flat surface (If you can, do Bhastrika Asana). Close your eyes and take deep breath thrice. Try to concentrate on the space between two eyebrows.This concentration point is called as Third Eye or Glabella point or Yintang point. The concentration point first visualizes a bright light in the Third eye point, slowly imagining you are entering that space and start visualizing the scene that is really happening in front of you.

That's it. These two techniques are really powerful and I,myself have experienced it. Dear reader, there are a lot of theories, practices and techniques that can help you train your mind. I strongly suggest and recommend that you follow any one of them with pure trust and belief. You'll definitely be super successful in your life.

I'd like to wrap up the lesson with a quote from one of my mentors, Praveen Wadalkar. He says, *"Only babies are born in this world"*. All humans have the same amount of 1300-1400 grams brain, nobody has special power. But if you resolute you can discover the true power within you and make yourself truly powerful.

Understand the TRUE POWER WITHIN YOU.

PAUSE REWIND PLAY...

CONGRATULATIONS...

Conclusion

I strongly believe that, a consequent 6 days of reading this book, as per the prescribed guidelines would have strengthened the fundamentals of your positive thinking and enabled you to experience the hidden and untold secrets, than just reading it at a stretch.

In spite of numerous articles, books, motivations, education and trainings to attain the state of positive thinking and peaceful mind, still people throng for yet another source to find the same. BUT nothing has changed yet, WHY?

A string of differences define the winners and losers based on how they handle their mind, hence winners take control of their mind but losers allow their mind to control them.

"Unless you seal the hole in the bucket, you can't fill water in it."

So start again, nothing to loose; but will have a successful life.

About Author

Lucas Lenin has authored this fascinating book with a new vision of self-awareness which enables you to assess your personal and mental health status equally. Determined self-awareness enables us identify the gaps and strategize them to obtain peaceful mind, while eliminating the negativity from us, hence; we become consciously more successful with wide range of positive vibes and self-realization.

The author is an entrepreneur, a life coach and a professional trainer with a decade and 8 years of experience. In his tenure he has enabled many people to reach the state of financial freedom. He also has rich experience in corporate industries like automotive, printing of packaging, lubricants, electronics etc.,. He has been successful in various businesses like E-learning, retails, agricultures, logistics, real estate and digital marketing.

His passion is "learning and coaching". He has conducted 100 + trainings and helped thousands of people to develop their knowledge in core fields. As the author I, Lucas Lenin kindly welcome you to march with me, "to learn more, achieve more and live happiest life"

Printed by Libri Plureos GmbH in Hamburg, Germany